Life in the Stone Age

By Deborah Lock

US Senior Editor Shannon Beatty
Assistant Editor Prerna Grewal
Senior Art Editor Ann Cannings
Project Art Editor Rashika Kachroo
Art Editor Mohd Zishan
Jacket Coordinator Francesca Young
Jacket Designers Amy Keast, Suzena Sengupta
DTP Designers Nand Kishor Acharya, Anita Yadav
Picture Researcher Nishwan Rasool
Producer, Pre-Production Rob Dunn
Producer Niamh Tierney
Managing Editors Deborah Lock, Monica Saigal
Managing Art Editor Diane Peyton Jones
Deputy Managing Art Editor Ivy Sengupta
Art Director Martin Wilson
Publisher Sarah Larter
Publishing Director Sophie Mitchell

Reading Consultant Linda Gambrell
Subject Consultant James Dilley

First American Edition, 2018
Published in the United States by DK Publishing
345 Hudson Street, New York, New York 10014

Published in Great Britain by Dorling Kindersley Limited

A catalog record for this book is available from the Library of Congress.
ISBN: 978-1-4654-6845-1 (Paperback)
ISBN: 978-1-4654-6846-8 (Hardcover)

DK books are available at special discounts when purchased in bulk
for sales promotions, premiums, fund-raising, or educational use.
For details, contact: DK Publishing Special Markets,
345 Hudson Street, New York, New York 10014
SpecialSales@dk.com
Printed and bound in China

The publisher would like to thank the following for their kind permission to reproduce their photographs:
(Key: a-above; b-below/bottom; c-center; f-far; l-left; r-right; t-top)
1 123RF.com: Adrian Wojcik. **4–5 123RF.com:** Natalia Lukiyanova (background). **5 Dorling Kindersley:** Royal Pavilion & Museums,
Brighton & Hove (clb). **6–7 iStockphoto.com:** Kdgeisler (b). **12–13 123RF.com:** Guillermo Avello; Gleb Semenov (background).
14 123RF.com: Raldi Somers (cl). **15 Dreamstime.com:** Isselee (bl). **16 Dorling Kindersley:** Royal Pavilion & Museums, Brighton &
Hove (c). **18–19 Dreamstime.com:** Alanjeffery. **22 Dorling Kindersley:** Pitt Rivers Museum, University of Oxford (cr); Royal Pavilion
& Museums, Brighton & Hove (clb). **25 123RF.com:** Pixphoto. **26 123RF.com:** Kalcutta (c). **27 123RF.com:** PaylessImages (cr).
28 Klint Janulis: (clb). **29 Klint Janulis.** **32–33 123RF.com:** Rcaucino. **35 123RF.com:** Adrian Wojcik. **37 Getty Images:** Universal
History Archive. **38–39 iStockphoto.com:** Nicolamargaret. **40–41 123RF.com:** Arindam Banerjee (background).
Dorling Kindersley: Dan Crisp (all). **42–43 123RF.com:** Дмитрий Гооль (Dmitry Gool). **44–45 123RF.com:** jetfoto

Jacket images: Front: **123RF.com:** Arindam Banerjee; **Dorling Kindersley:** Royal Pavilion & Museums,
Brighton & Hove br, Science Museum, London cra

All other images © Dorling Kindersley
For further information see: www.dkimages.com

A WORLD OF IDEAS:
SEE ALL THERE IS TO KNOW

www.dk.com

Contents

The Stone Age

The Stone Age is the time when the first people lived.

Old Stone Age
3.3 million–11,500
years ago

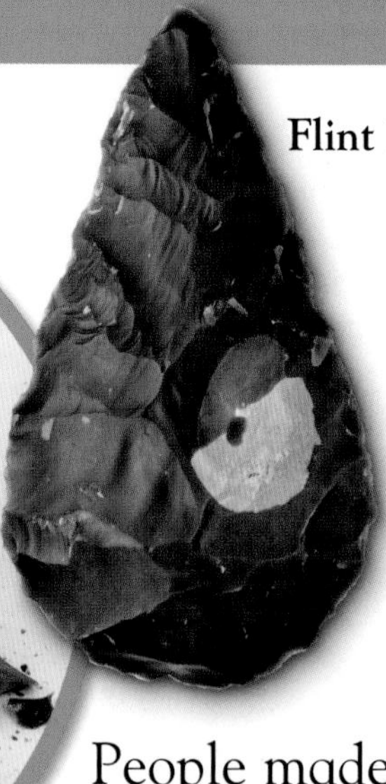

Flint hand ax

People made tools for cutting meat.

Harpoon tips

People made
new tools such
as harpoon tips
from deer antlers.

| Middle Stone Age 11,500–6,500 years ago | New Stone Age 6,500–4,000 years ago |

Polished ax head

People became
farmers, but still
used tools made
from stone.

Chapter 1
Setting up camp

Ice covered large parts of the world at times in the Stone Age. Early people had to find ways to survive the cold.

People moved camps each season. They had to gather plants and hunt animals to eat and make tools. They followed the animals so that they could hunt them.

Animals such as deer moved from place to place to find food.

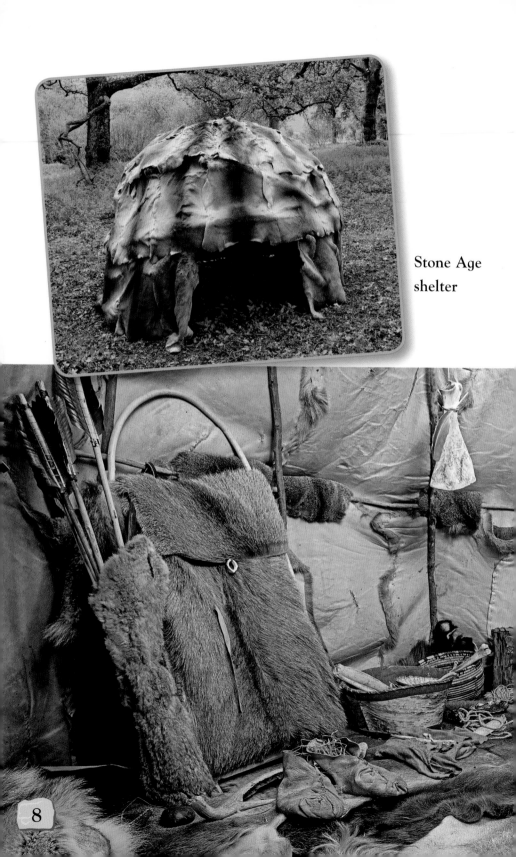

Stone Age shelter

People needed good shelters to
live in. The frames were made from
thin tree branches. These were
covered in animal skins, grass,
or tree bark. This kept the inside
of the shelters warm and dry.

Animal skins covered
the floor to keep the
inside snug.

People wore clothes to keep warm. Deerskin was softened to make leather. Tunics and pants were made from leather or plants.

Fur tunics were worn for hunting in winter. Fur shoes were filled with grasses for extra warmth.

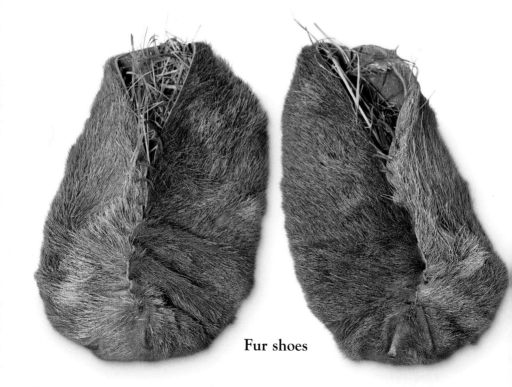

Fur shoes

Stone Age house

This New Stone Age
house had a grass roof.
Let's look inside.

Skara Brae,
Orkney Islands, UK

Key

1. Wall of stacked flat stones
2. Fire pit
3. Stone shelves
4. Stone bed

Chapter 2
On the hunt

Early people hunted all sorts
of animals. They caught fish
and other animals in rivers.
They trapped birds.

Ptarmigan

Fish

Seal

They hunted small animals like frogs and hares. There were also wild horses, wild boars, and deer to hunt.

Frog

Brown hare

Deer

Wild boar

People needed good tools to catch the animals. They made tools out of wood, stone, bone, antlers, and shells. The tools had sharp points to cut through the animal skin.

A fishing spear is also known as a harpoon.

Hunters waded in rivers to spear fish.

Stone Age people went hunting with dogs. They fed and tamed wolf cubs. These became the first dogs.

These tamed wolves also guarded the camps. They kept away dangerous wild animals like bears.

The large land animals like mammoths were dangerous to hunt. Stone Age hunters were brave. They learned to throw long spears very fast and very far.

Spears were made from wood with stone or antler tips.

Every part of an animal was used—tusks and bones for tools, fur skin for clothes, and the meat was eaten.

Stone Age tools

Stone Age people made tools
for different jobs. They used
tools to hunt, cut trees down,
and chop meat.

Hand axes were
used to cut meat.

A pebble hammer
helped to make
ax blades.

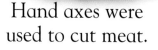

People used flint
blades to cut plants.

People hunted and fished using a spear.

Stone

A digging stick was used to plant crops.

Wood

Axes were used to cut trees down.

Chapter 3
Into the forest

Stone Age people did not just eat meat. They gathered plants such as fruits, nuts, and roots.

Blackberries

Radishes

Hazelnuts

People knew which plants were good and which ones made them sick.

Greater burdock has a prickly flower head.

People also used plants for medicines. Some roots and leaves kept them healthy. They soaked burdock roots in hot water to make warm drinks.

Nettle leaves

Willow bark

Burdock roots

They added nettle leaves to soups. The bark of a willow helped to stop pain.

People used bark from trees to make buckets. They used these buckets to carry and store food and water. They wove flexible branches into baskets to trap fish.

Tree bark containers

Fish-catching basket

They wove long grass into roofs.
Rainwater ran down the outside
to keep the inside dry.

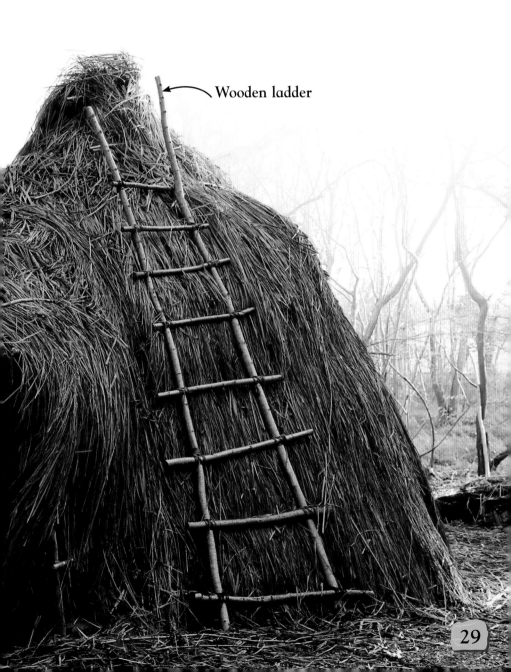

Wooden ladder

Making fire

1 Dried grass / Dry sticks

2 Bow / Drill

3 Smoke

4 Small flames

Early people learned how to make fire. Small dry sticks, dried grass, and a bow drill were used.

They used the fire to cook food and keep warm. Fire also gave them light to work in the evening. Wild animals were scared of fire and stayed away.

Fire pit

Making rope

Early people made
rope from thin,
strong plant stems.
They used the rope
to make traps
and sew clothes.

Nettle
leaves
sting

You will need:
nettle plant

1. Strip the
leaves from
the stem.

2. Crush the stem with a thumb to soften it.

3. Strip away the outer layer and leave to dry.

4. Twist some outer layers together to make the rope.

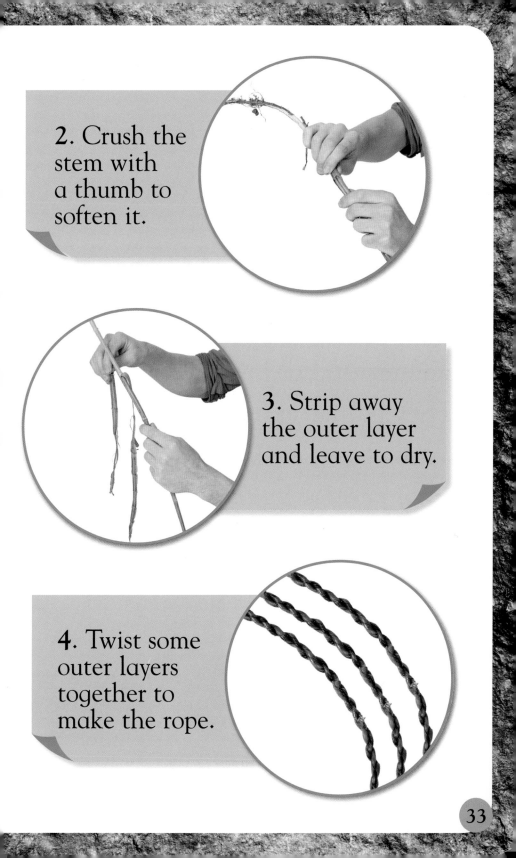

Chapter 4
Celebrations

Early people used caves as
shelters and as meeting places.
They painted pictures on the
walls. They used red, yellow, and
brown colors found in the soil.
The black color came from burned
wood, called charcoal.

Crushed red
rock in shell

Yellow
rock pebble

Charcoal

These hand paintings are in Argentina.

Stone Age people believed in good and bad spirits. They drew the animals that they hunted on the cave walls. They may have been asking the animal spirits for good luck when hunting.

Shamans were people who led these rituals.

These cave paintings
are in France.

Some special places were marked with huge stones. These may have been meeting places for special days of the year.

Lots of people may have met together on the shortest day of the year. The stones at Stonehenge allow the setting sun to shine through.

Stonehenge is in the south of England, UK.

What came next?

People started to live in one place at the end of the Stone Age. They kept small farms to grow crops and raise animals.

Can you find these things in the picture:

Pigs · Cattle · Farmer

Sower · Crops · Goats

Quiz

 1 In which part of the Stone Age did people become farmers?

 2 What was leather made of?

 3 What were used to make the frames for shelters?

 4 Which animals became the first dogs?

 5 Which tool was used to plant crops in the Stone Age?

6 Which leaves were added to soups in the Stone Age?

 7 What did people in the Stone Age use to stop pain?

 8 What was needed to make a fire in the Stone Age?

 9 Who led the rituals?

 10 What is charcoal?

Answers on page 45

Glossary

bark
hard outer covering of a tree

bow drill
small bow and a wooden drill used
to make fire in the Stone Age

crop
plants grown in large amounts

flint
hard stone used for tools in the
Stone Age

frame
firm, strong shape

harpoon
long spear with a pointed end

leather
material made from animal skin

mammoths
large animal with thick fur and
long curved tusks

medicine
something used to treat illness

ritual
ceremony with a set of actions

season
winter, spring, summer, or fall

shaman
person believed to have powers
to heal people and speak to spirits

shelters
covered place for people to live in
for a short time

sower
person who scatters seeds in a field

tunic
piece of knee-length clothing

Answers to the quiz:

1. New Stone Age; 2. Animal skin; 3. Thin branches;
4. Wolves; 5. Digging stick; 6. Nettle leaves; 7. Willow
bark; 8. Small dry sticks, dried grass, and a bow drill;
9. Shamans; 10. Burned wood

Guide for Parents

This book is part of an exciting four-level reading series for children, developing the habit of reading widely for both pleasure and information. These chapter books have a compelling main narrative to suit your child's reading ability. Each book is designed to develop your child's reading skills, fluency, grammar awareness, and comprehension in order to build confidence and engagement when reading.

Ready for a *Level 2* book

YOUR CHILD SHOULD

- be familiar with using beginning letter sounds and context clues to figure out unfamiliar words.
- be aware of the need for a slight pause at commas and a longer one at periods.
- alter his/her expression for questions and exclamations.

A VALUABLE AND SHARED READING EXPERIENCE

For many children, reading requires much effort, but adult participation can make this both fun and easier. So here are a few tips on how to use this book with your child.

TIP 1 Check out the contents together before your child begins:
- read the text about the book on the back cover.
- flip through the book and stop to chat about the contents page together to heighten your child's interest and expectation.
- make use of unfamiliar or difficult words on the page in a brief discussion.
- chat about the nonfiction reading features used in the book, such as headings, captions, or labels.

TIP 2 Support your child as he/she reads the story pages:

- give the book to your child to read and turn the pages.

- where necessary, encourage your child to break a word into syllables, sound out each one, and then flow the syllables together. Ask him/her to reread the sentence to check the meaning.

- you may need to help read some new vocabulary words that are difficult for your child to sound out.

- when there's a question mark or an exclamation point, encourage your child to vary his/her voice as he/she reads the sentence. Demonstrate how to do this if it is helpful.

TIP 3 Talk at the end of each page:

- ask questions about the text and the meaning of the words used. These help to develop comprehension skills and awareness of the language used.

A FEW ADDITIONAL TIPS

- Always encourage your child to try reading difficult words by themselves. Praise any self-corrections, for example, "I like the way you sounded out that word and then changed the way you said it, to make sense."

- Try to read together everyday. Reading little and often is best. These books are divided into manageable chapters for one reading session. However, after 10 minutes, only keep going if your child wants to read on.

- Read other books of different types to your child just for enjoyment and information.

Series consultant, **Dr. Linda Gambrell,** Distinguished Professor of Education at Clemson University, has served as President of the National Reading Conference, the College Reading Association, and the International Reading Association.

Index